PET FINDERS
Underground

Written by Margaret Ryan
Illustrated by Shahab Shamshirsaz

Published by Pearson Education Limited, Edinburgh Gate, Harlow, Essex, CM20 2JE.

www.pearsonschools.co.uk

Text © Margaret Ryan 2013

Designed by Bigtop
Original illustrations © Pearson Education 2013
Illustrated by Shahab Shamshirsaz, Sylvie Poggio

The right of Margaret Ryan to be identified as author of this work has been asserted by her in accordance with the Copyright, Designs and Patents Act 1988.

First published 2013

17 16 15 14 13
10 9 8 7 6 5 4 3 2 1

British Library Cataloguing in Publication Data
A catalogue record for this book is available from the British Library

ISBN 978 0 435 14365 7

Copyright notice
All rights reserved. No part of this publication may be reproduced in any form or by any means (including photocopying or storing it in any medium by electronic means and whether or not transiently or incidentally to some other use of this publication) without the written permission of the copyright owner, except in accordance with the provisions of the Copyright, Designs and Patents Act 1988 or under the terms of a licence issued by the Copyright Licensing Agency, Saffron House, 6–10 Kirby Street, London EC1N 8TS (www.cla.co.uk). Applications for the copyright owner's written permission should be addressed to the publisher.

Printed in Malaysia, CTP-PJB

Acknowledgements
We would like to thank Bangor Central Integrated Primary School, Northern Ireland; Bishop Henderson Church of England Primary School, Somerset; Bletchingdon Parochial Church of England Primary School, Oxfordshire; Brookside Community Primary School, Somerset; Bude Park Primary School, Hull; Cheddington Combined School, Buckinghamshire; Dair House Independent School, Buckinghamshire; Glebe Infant School, Gloucestershire; Henley Green Primary School, Coventry; Lovelace Primary School, Surrey; Our Lady of Peace Junior School, Slough; Tackley Church of England Primary School, Oxfordshire; and Twyford Church of England School, Buckinghamshire for their invaluable help in the development and trialling of the Bug Club resources.

Every effort has been made to contact copyright holders of material reproduced in this book. Any omissions will be rectified in subsequent printings if notice is given to the publishers.

Chapter One

It was the summer holidays but Amelia and Rory were as miserable as a grey day in November.

"My mum says we can't afford to go away on holiday this year," muttered Amelia, as she sat on the low wall between their houses.

"My dad said the same," said Rory, kicking a ball against the wall. "There's no money to pay me to do the chores either. I'm totally broke."

"Me too," moaned Amelia. "I checked this morning and my money box is completely empty."

They both sighed deeply.

"I guess there's no use complaining. There's nothing we can do about it," shrugged Rory.

"Unless …" Amelia was suddenly thoughtful, "… unless we set up our own business."

"Our own business?" Rory echoed.

But Amelia wasn't listening; she had already started planning. "The first thing we must do is make a list of what we're good at. Wait here."

Rory did as he was told, while Amelia ran into the house and came back with two pieces of paper and two pencils. "There. Write down what you think I'm good at and I'll do the same for you," Amelia ordered.

Rory screwed up his face and thought for a moment. Then he wrote:

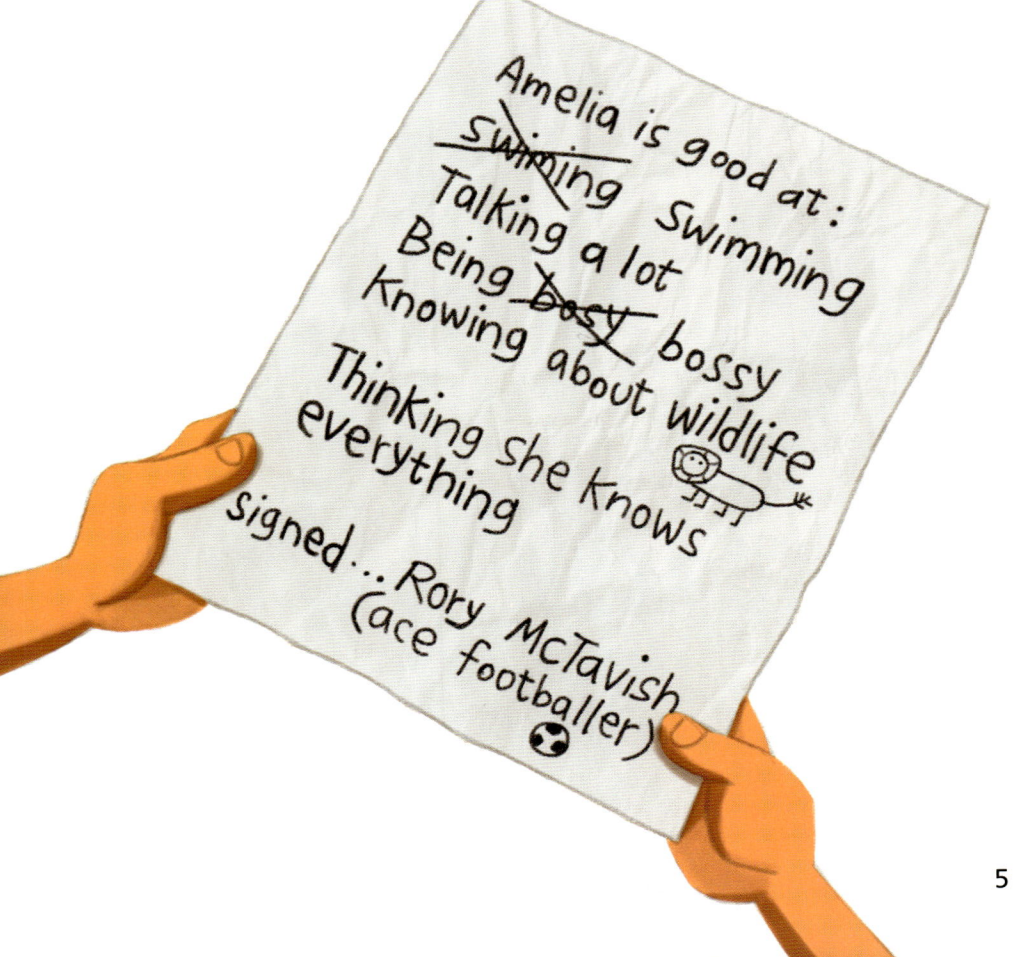

Amelia didn't have to think. Straight away she wrote down:

Rory is good at:
Football
Telling terrible jokes
Being silly
Burping loudly
Signed...
Miss Amelia Fudge, aged 9

They showed each other what they had written, and neither of them was very impressed.

"Well, that wasn't much help," said Rory. "And my jokes aren't terrible."

"And I'm not bossy," said Amelia, looking at the lists again and shaking her head. "There must be something we can do," she muttered.

"Think, Rory!"

They were both having a serious think when old Mrs Collins from across the road stopped to ask if they'd seen a one-eyed cat wearing a tartan collar.

"Nelson's always wandering off," she said, "but he's not usually away for this long. I'm really worried that something may have happened to him this time."

Amelia jumped up, her eyes suddenly gleaming. "Stop worrying right now, Mrs Collins," she declared. "You've come to the right place! Rory and I have just formed the … Pet Finders Agency! We will be happy to take on your case."

"The wha ... Pet Finders Agency? Case?" spluttered Rory.

Amelia ignored him and continued. "It's our new business venture to earn some pocket money," she explained to Mrs Collins. "We're especially good at finding lost cats."

"In that case I'd be very happy to leave it up to you to look for him," said Mrs Collins. "Your young legs are much faster than mine." With that she wandered off down the road.

"Amelia ..." Rory began, but Amelia wasn't listening.

"Let's get started straight away," she said. "We need to advertise our services. You do a poster to put in the village shop window and I'll do some leaflets. We can deliver them while we look for Nelson. And change out of those awful shorts and into some suitable clothes. The Pet Finders must look professional."

Rory stood to attention and gave a comic salute. "Anything else, Your Majesty?"

"Yes. Stop being so silly," frowned Amelia.

"Then stop being so bossy," said Rory.

But Amelia was already hurrying inside; there was work to be done.

Chapter Two

An hour later, Amelia was ready for action. She wore her best black jeans, black trainers and a white T-shirt on which she had stencilled PFA. On her belt she hung a small torch, a short length of rope and her mobile phone, and she carried the leaflets she had made in a canvas rucksack slung over her shoulder. She looked at herself in the hall mirror. "Pretty cool." She smiled at her reflection before heading outside to wait for Rory.

She didn't have to wait for long. A few minutes later Rory appeared in the garden wearing his oldest T-shirt and jeans, a cycle helmet, knee and elbow pads and camouflage paint.

"What are you wearing all that for?" she exclaimed. "You look ridiculous!"

"Catching Nelson could be dangerous," said Rory. "He might be up a tree somewhere for all you know!"

Amelia was not convinced. "We'd better get going," she said. "We'll search all the front gardens first and deliver the leaflets at the same time. Where's your poster for the shop window?"

Rory reached into his back pocket and proudly pulled out a folded piece of paper. He had used his special three-coloured pen to write it.

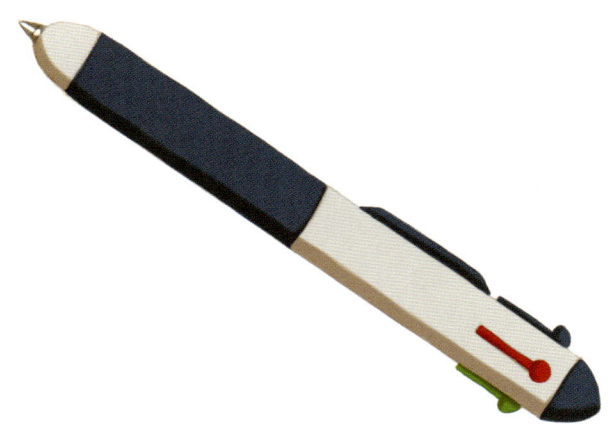

NEW BUSINESS IN TOWN

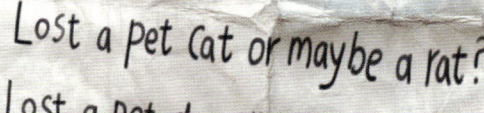
Lost a pet cat or maybe a rat?

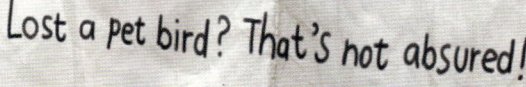
Lost a pet dog or maybe a frog?

Lost a pet bird? That's not absured!

Lost a pet bunny? Now that isn't funny!

Lost a pet llama? Gosh what a drama!

Lost a pet goat? Got a lump in your throat?

Then please don't despair,
for help is at hand
in the shape of PET FINDERS,
the best in the land!

For prompt and speedy service Contract
R McTavish on 072

"I've put my dad's mobile number on it," explained Rory.

"I've put my mum's on the leaflets," said Amelia, secretly wishing she'd done her leaflets in colour and in rhyme. "Come on. We'll start by checking our own gardens."

After looking in the flower borders, they checked through the sheds in their back gardens. All they found were broken pots, rusty lawn mowers and spiders' webs.

"I hate spiders' webs," muttered Amelia, as she pulled bits from her hair.

"Should have worn a crash helmet," grinned Rory.

Next, they worked their way along the street. They carefully checked through the front gardens of the houses on their street, peering over the walls and fences.

"Some of these have a lot of junk," sniffed Amelia. "Haven't the owners ever heard of recycling?" Rory just shook his head.

Finally, they checked through all the bins. "Cor! What a pong!" said Rory, holding his nose. "I should have worn a face mask as well."

"This is useless – Nelson's not here," Amelia said. "Let's go into the village shop and ask if we can put up your poster."

Mrs McNeil, the shop owner, was very helpful when they told her about the Pet Finders Agency.

"What a good idea," she smiled. "You can put your poster in the window beside the one that says 'Bagpipes for sale'."

"Where do we go now?" asked Rory.

"We'll try the park," said Amelia. "Nelson's probably there."

"No, he's not!" cried Rory, as he grabbed her arm and pointed. "I've just seen him go into that garden. Come on, follow me!"

Amelia hurried after Rory as he raced back up the street and into the garden of number thirty-two.

"Gotcha," he yelled, as he pounced on a one-eyed cat wearing a tartan collar.

The cat miaowed loudly and struggled in Rory's arms.

"Put him in here," said Amelia, holding open her bag.

Rory was putting the cat into the bag just as the front door flew open.

"Thieves! Robbers! Put my cat down this minute!"

Amelia and Rory stared at the strange woman who stood in the doorway.

"Your cat? But this is Nelson, Mrs Collins's cat. She asked us to find him and take him home!" Amelia protested.

The woman came out and grabbed the cat from Amelia's bag. "This is most certainly not Nelson," she declared. "This is Jemima, and when I brought her with me to visit my sister, I did not expect to encounter catnappers!"

"We're not catnappers. We're Pet Finders," argued Amelia, but the woman just glared and whisked the cat back indoors.

Amelia scowled at Rory. "This is not a good start for the Pet Finders Agency."

Rory shrugged at her. "Well, how was I to know there would be two one-eyed cats wearing tartan collars?"

Chapter Three

Amelia and Rory headed for the park to continue their search for Nelson.

"Let's look in the play area first," said Rory, but Amelia shook her head.

"We're not here to play on the swings, Rory, and Nelson's not likely to be whizzing round on the roundabout."

Rory made a face. He could swing much higher than Amelia. They continued their search in the bushes, but they only found an empty crisp packet and a cola can. There was no sign of Nelson.

"Ow!" cried Amelia angrily, as she scratched her leg on a spiky bush.

"You should have worn knee pads," grinned Rory.

Next they searched around all the trees, calling out, "Nelson! Nelson! Where are you?" But he was nowhere to be found. They did, however, disturb a pigeon which landed a dropping on Amelia's arm.

"Yuk," she cried, wiping it off.

"You should have worn elbow pads," said Rory, chuckling. Amelia glared at him.

They carried on looking for some time, but after checking all the obvious places they still couldn't find Nelson.

"This is harder work than I thought," said Rory. "I wonder where he's got to. We've looked everywhere!"

"Not everywhere," said Amelia. "We haven't tried the loch side yet."

"You don't think he's gone for a swim, do you?" said Rory. "I thought cats didn't like water much."

"Don't be silly," said Amelia. "He could be caught up in some fishing lines or have slipped on the rocks and hurt himself. There are all sorts of hazards!"

"Then we'd better go and look," cried Rory, and he charged off shouting, "Pet Finders to the rescue!"

Amelia grinned and ran after him.

They stopped running when they came to the loch side. They scrambled down the steep bank and stood looking at the familiar boats bobbing up and down. There was a larger one there that they didn't recognise, but all was quiet.

They tried calling Nelson again, but there was no response.

"Let's check under the upturned rowing boats," said Amelia. "Nelson could be trapped underneath."

It was hard work lifting the boats and by the time they'd finished propping them up, they were both out of breath. Apart from some pebbles, a few startled crabs and a starfish with a leg missing, they found nothing.

"I wonder how many places a cat could hide?" said Rory. "He's not on the beach. He's not on the rocks. He's not under the boats. Now we really have searched everywhere."

"Not quite everywhere," said Amelia. "We haven't searched the old sea cave yet."

"The old sea cave?" cried Rory. "We can't search there. My dad says it might be haunted! People have heard strange noises coming from it – moanings and groanings, creakings and wailings. There's no way I'm going in there!"

"Why not?" said Amelia, indignantly. "Aren't we the fearless Pet Finders? How can we earn pocket money if we can't face up to danger? Are you a man or a mouse, Rory McTavish?"

"Squeak," shivered Rory in reply.

Chapter Four

Amelia hurried along the beach towards the old sea cave. Rory picked up a heavy piece of driftwood and reluctantly followed her.

A large black cloud slid over the sun and fat drops of rain began to fall as they scrambled over rocks, slimy with seaweed. When they finally rounded the headland, the old sea cave came into view. Its entrance was a gaping black hole in the cliff, dark and mysterious.

"I don't like it," said Rory, as a rumble of thunder made them jump.

"Me neither," admitted Amelia, "but we've come this far, so we'll just take a quick look."

The words were hardly out of her mouth when they heard a faint noise.

"Oh no, it's the start of the moaning and groaning," said Rory, fearing the worst.

"Don't be silly," frowned Amelia. "Just be quiet and listen."

They stood very still, hardly daring to breathe. The faint sound came again.

"I'm sure that's a cat mewing," said Amelia.

"Or a ghost … " quivered Rory.

"Come on," said Amelia. "We're the Pet Finders; it's our duty to find out."

Rory followed her and cautiously they made their way towards the cave. As they approached, Amelia noticed marks in the sand.

"Paw prints!" she cried, pointing to the damp sand. "That's our first clue."

"Footprints too," said Rory nervously.

"Well, surely there can't be real catnappers around," frowned Amelia. "What would they want with poor old Nelson?"

They crept forward towards the cave. In front of them, the entrance loomed large and forbidding but as they approached, the faint noise grew stronger.

"It *is* a cat," said Amelia. The thunder rumbled and the light grew dim as they entered the cave. Amelia removed her torch from her belt and switched it on. They could plainly hear the mewing now.

"He's somewhere nearby," she whispered.

"Why are you whispering?" whispered Rory.

"I don't know. Why are you?" Amelia whispered back. "Anyway, I think the noise is coming from over there." She swung her torch towards the cave wall, and after a moment or two, its beam picked up one bright green eye.

"It's Nelson!" she cried.

It was Nelson all right and he was trapped. His tartan collar was caught on a rusted metal spike sticking out of the cave wall.

"You poor thing," said Amelia gently, and, giving the torch to Rory, she freed the cat.

"Poor old Nelson," she soothed. "We'll soon have you back home. I'll pop you into my bag so you'll be safe while we're climbing back …"

"Shush, Amelia," whispered Rory sharply, interrupting her. "I thought I heard something."

"What?" said Amelia impatiently. "We've got Nelson now. You're not on about ghosts again, are you?"

"Ghosts don't leave footprints. I think there's someone else here. Look."

Rory pointed the torch at the cave floor where footprints showed up clearly in the sand heading deeper into the cave.

Amelia looked at the floor. "There are two sets of footprints," she whispered. "I wonder who they belong to?"

"There's only one way to find out," said Rory, grasping his stick more tightly.

"Okay," agreed Amelia. "But we have to be careful …"

Nelson settled down and nodded off to sleep in Amelia's bag as they made their way further into the cave. Rory kept the torch pointing to the ground as they carefully followed the footprints.

"They're going off to the right," whispered Rory as they reached a junction in the tunnel. "I wonder what's around that corner?"

"Keep close to the wall," warned Amelia. "Perhaps that way we can find out without being seen. It's probably just people exploring, but just in case …"

Chapter Five

Pressed against the cave wall, Amelia and Rory inched forward.

"Ow," cried Amelia, as Rory trod on her toe.

"Shush," instructed Rory, "and listen. I can hear a funny clicking noise and yapping."

"That doesn't sound like people exploring the cave to me," said Amelia, suddenly feeling anxious. "Perhaps we should go back."

"No, not when we've come this far," said Rory. "Anyway, I've got my stick ..."

They inched forward a bit further as the cave opened out and sloped downwards. Then the cave wall rounded another bend and a faint glow appeared. This time, amidst the clicking and yapping, Amelia and Rory could hear men's voices. They sneaked up closer and listened.

"Can't you keep these things quiet?" said one. "We don't want to attract any attention."

"You worry too much," said the other. "No one ever comes here. Not since I spread the rumour in the village that this place was haunted."

The first man laughed. "That was a good idea. But I wish the buyers would hurry up and come to collect them. They keep snapping at me."

"They're in cages. They can't do you any harm, and the truck can't come till later. We have to wait till it's dark to do the transfer. Relax. Everything's fine. Once this delivery's made, we'll have loads of cash and we can sail away and spend it."

"That's the bit I like," the first man laughed.

Amelia and Rory looked at each other. What had they stumbled on? Then Amelia's hand touched something metal. She drew it back quickly as she heard a scuffling sound.

"I think I touched one of the cages," she whispered to Rory. "There's something in it, but I don't know what."

"I'll cover the torch with my hand so it doesn't give off much light and we can have a quick look," whispered Rory. He covered the torch so that only a faint beam showed.

"Over here," whispered Amelia. "This is where I touched the metal."

Rory shone the torch and a creature with two bright eyes blinked back at him. He shone the torch down the creature's body till it came to a long stripy tail.

"I'm sure that's a lemur," Amelia said quietly. "They're from Madagascar. They're threatened with extinction. I've read all about it. By the sound of it, these men have stolen them and are selling them on."

"Right," said Rory, formulating a plan. "They don't know we're here, so we can surprise them. I'll charge in and tackle them with my stick while you rescue the lemurs."

Amelia shook her head and stared at Rory in disbelief. "That's far too dangerous."

"But I'm wearing my crash helmet, elbow and knee pads," protested Rory.

"No. It's still too dangerous," insisted Amelia. "We'll sneak back out and phone the police. My mobile won't work this deep in the cave. Now come on before we're spotted."

"Okay ..." muttered Rory, but as he turned to follow Amelia, his stick caught the lemur cages and tipped them over.

"Oh no," he gasped, as the cage doors flew open. The lemurs leapt out and swiftly headed towards the faint light where the men were.

"Er ... I think you're right, Amelia. I think we need to get out of here right now!"

Chapter Six

Amelia and Rory made their way back outside as fast as they could, and while Rory kept an eye on the cave mouth, Amelia ran a little way from the cave and phoned the police.

"This is Amelia Fudge of the Pet Finders Agency," she said, breathlessly. "I wish to report a major crime."

"Well?" asked Rory, when she'd finished on the phone.

"The police will be here shortly, but we've to stay well clear. 'Go home' was what the policeman said."

"And miss all the fun? No way," said Rory. "We found the criminals. We're the real Pet Finders. Anyway, they might hear the police arriving and try to escape …".

"You're right." Amelia frowned. "But there is something we could do to delay them." She untied the rope at her waist. "Take one end of the rope and go to the far side of the cave entrance. I'll go to the other. We'll stretch the rope across and bury it in the sand, keeping hold of the ends. That way, we can hide round the side of the cave and if the men try to escape we can pull on the rope and trip them up."

"Good idea," agreed Rory.

He helped to bury the rope, and when it was well covered with sand, they took up their positions and waited.

Soon, several police cars and a dog handler's van could be seen racing along the loch side. Within minutes the police were on the beach and clambering over the rocks, but the rocks were slippery and the policemen's boots found it hard to get a grip. Then a police helicopter appeared, its rotor blades whirring noisily.

Amelia looked straight at Rory. The men were bound to hear that.

She saw Rory thinking the same thing. They gave each other the thumbs-up sign and held tightly onto the ends of the rope.

"Now!" they cried, as the men came running out of the cave with lemurs clinging to them.

The rope shot up and the men yelled as they fell over it onto the sand. The lemurs leapt away to the safety of the nearby rocks.

Two seconds later a growling police dog was standing over the criminals. Then the men were surrounded by police.

Amelia and Rory let go of the rope and grinned at each other.

Amelia explained all about Nelson and the Pet Finders Agency to the inspector as the rest of the police officers captured the lemurs on the rocks and then went into the cave to rescue the others.

"Well done, Pet Finders," smiled the inspector. "We've been on the lookout for these guys for some time. Unfortunately, there's quite a trade in endangered species like lemurs. And, who knows, there might even be a reward for their return."

Amelia smiled and suddenly remembered why they'd come to the cave in the first place.

"That reminds me," she said. "We must go and return Nelson to Mrs Collins."

Nelson who had slept through all the excitement, opened his one sleepy eye and miaowed in agreement.